*Wesley Schaum's*

# TUNES for TWO
## BOOK ONE

T0065891

## • • • FOREWORD • • •

A great music educator once said, "Rhythm is caught, not taught." Duet playing provides valuable experience developing a sense of rhythm.

These duets are designed for two students at the same level – primo and secondo parts are of *equal difficulty*. Both parts are fun to learn because both players are given interesting accompaniments as well as melodies.

It is suggested that a student alternate parts, learning the primo part for one piece, the secondo part for the next, etc. This gives valuable sight-reading experience with both hands in treble clef and with both hands in bass clef.

Duet playing provides an excellent opportunity for *ear training*. Emphasis should be placed on *listening carefully* to both parts so that the melody can be heard clearly and the accompaniment subdued.

Used in recital programs, duets add variety, audience appeal and showmanship.

## • • • INDEX • • •

EXCLUSIVELY DISTRIBUTED BY

HAL•LEONARD®
CORPORATION
7777 W. BLUEMOUND RD. P.O. BOX 13819 MILWAUKEE, WI 53213

© Copyright 1963 by Schaum Publications, Inc., Mequon, Wisconsin
International Copyright Secured • All Rights Reserved • Printed in U.S.A.

05-71
AR-22

# Glow Worm

*Secondo*

# Glow Worm

*Prímo*

Paul Lincke

# Frere Jacques (Brother John)

*Secondo*

Old French Folk Song

Allegretto

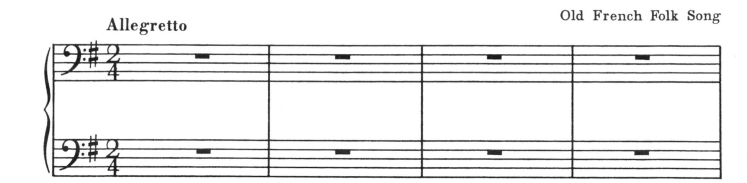

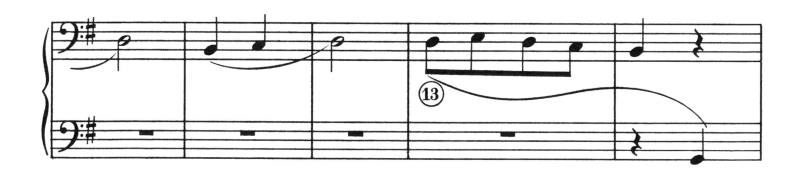

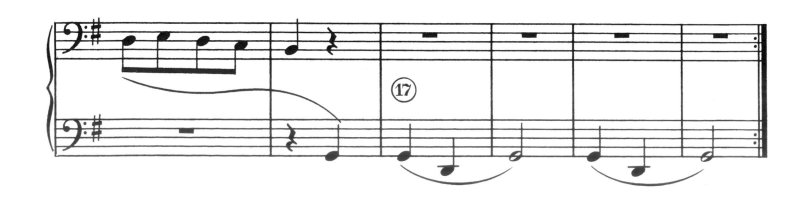

# Frere Jacques (Brother John)

*Prímo*

Allegretto

Old French Folk Song

# Whistler and His Dog

*Secondo*

Arthur Pryor

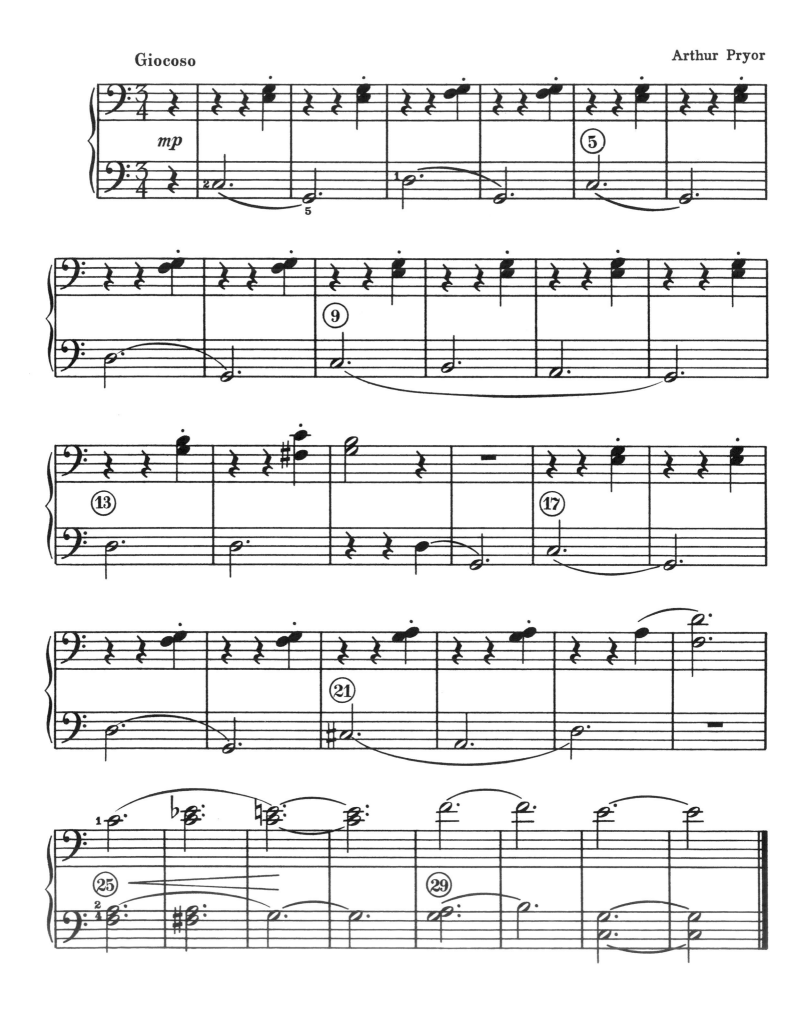

# Whistler and His Dog

Primo

Arthur Pryor

# On Top of Old Smoky

*Secondo*

Andante

American Mountain Tune

*rit.*

REMINDER: One secret of good duet playing is to PLAY THE ACCOMPANIMENT SOFTLY so that the melody can be heard easily. In order to achieve this, YOU MUST LISTEN CAREFULLY as you play.

# On Top of Old Smoky

Primo

American Mountain Tune

# American Patrol March

*Secondo*

F. W. Meacham

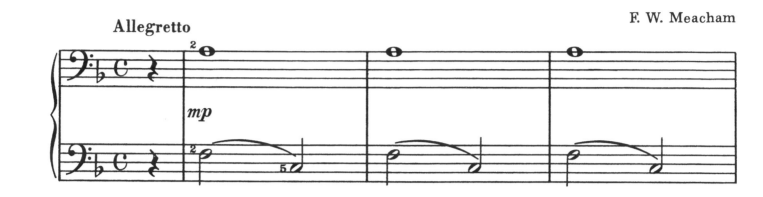

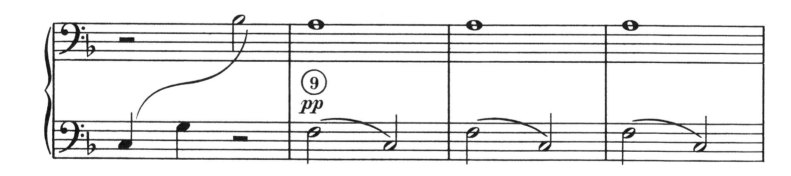

# American Patrol March

*Primo*

F. W. Meacham

# Pop! Goes the Weasel

*Secondo*

Allegretto

Traditional

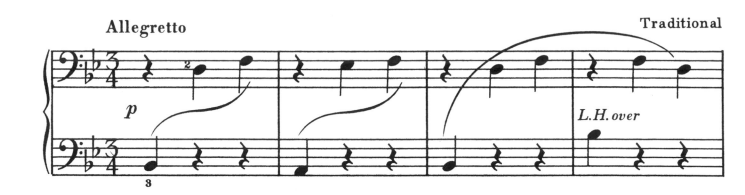

# Pop! Goes the Weasel

*Primo*

Traditional

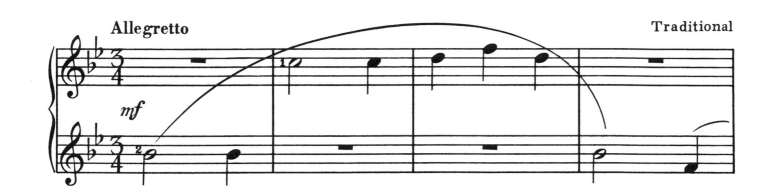

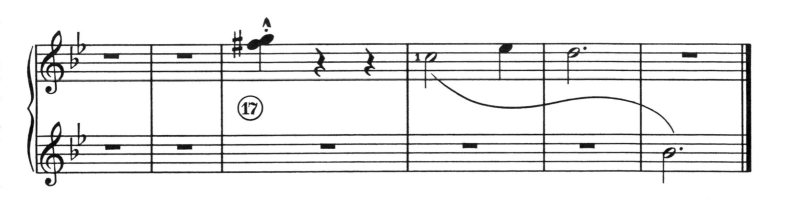

# Skip to My Lou

*Secondo*

American Folk Song

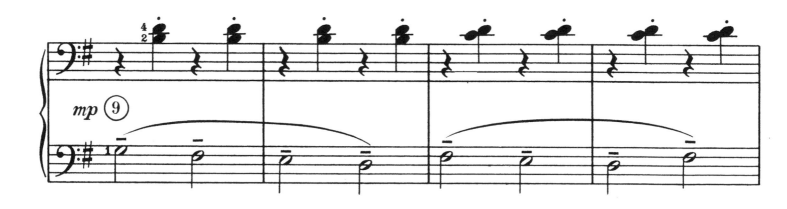

# Skip to My Lou

**Primo**

Vivace

American Folk Song

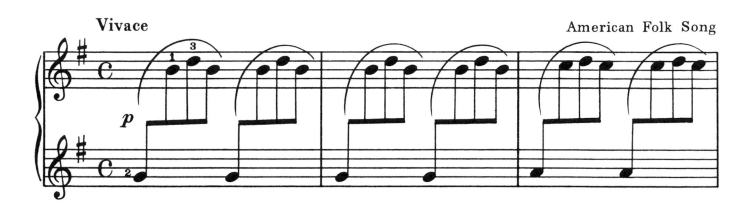

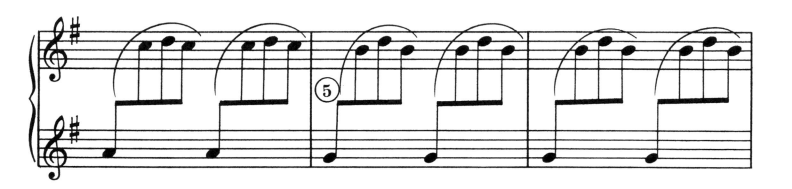

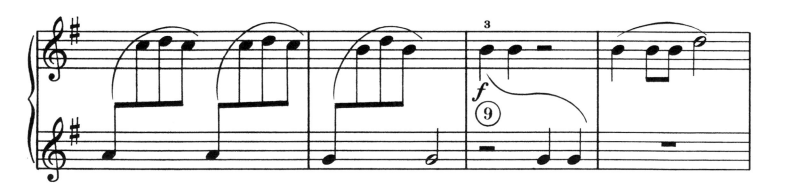

# Yellow Rose of Texas

*Secondo*

Traditional

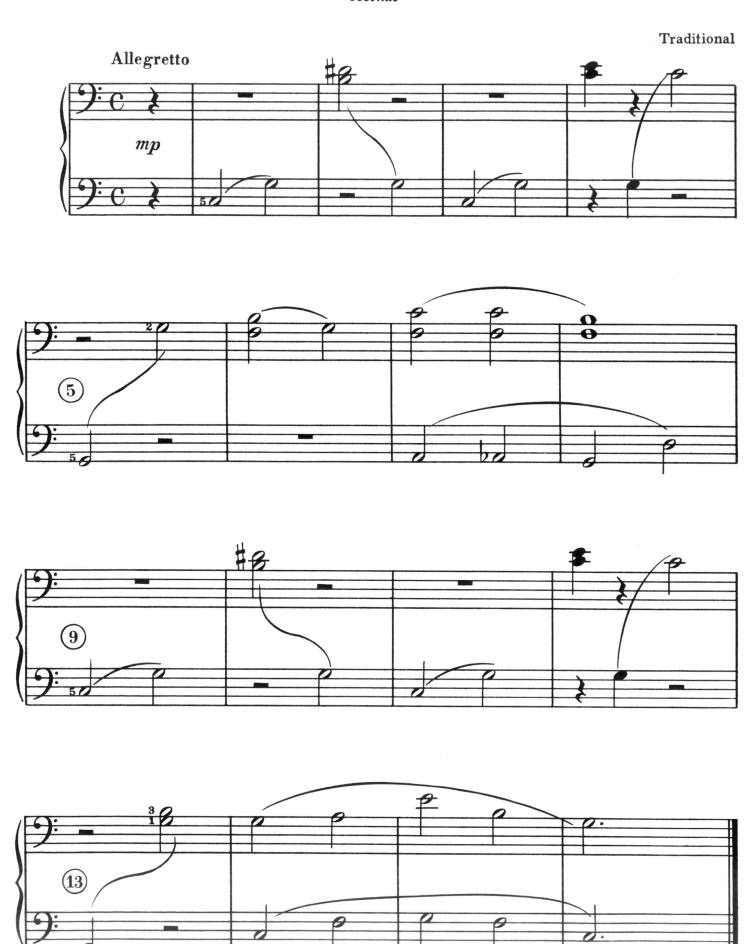

# Yellow Rose of Texas

*Primo*

Traditional

# Mexican Clap-Hands Dance

*Secondo*

Traditional

# Mexican Clap-Hands Dance

*Primo*

Traditional

# I've Been Workin' on the Railroad

*Secondo*

Traditional

REMINDER: One secret of good duet playing is to PLAY THE ACCOMPANIMENT SOFTLY so that the melody can be heard easily. In order to achieve this, YOU MUST LISTEN CAREFULLY as you play.

# I've Been Workin' on the Railroad

*Primo*

Traditional

REMINDER: One secret of good duet playing is to PLAY THE ACCOMPANIMENT SOFTLY so that the melody can be heard easily. In order to achieve this, YOU MUST LISTEN CAREFULLY as you play.

# Caissons Go Rolling Along

*Secondo*

Edmund L. Gruber

**Allegro moderato**

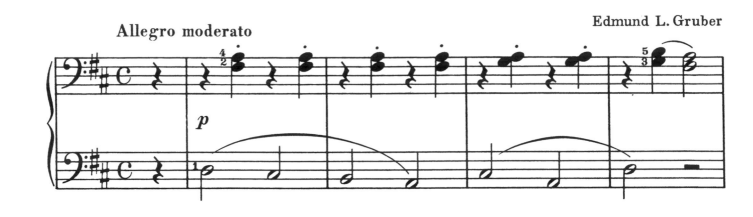

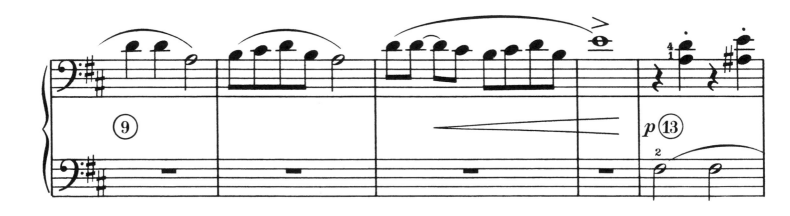

# Caissons Go Rolling Along

*Primo*

**Allegro moderato**

Edmund L. Gruber

# This Old Man

*Secondo*

# This Old Man

Primo

Allegretto

Traditional

# Little Dog Boogie

*Secondo*

Wesley Schaum

# Little Dog Boogie

Primo

Wesley Schaum

# Parade of the Toy Soldiers

*Secondo*

Tempo di Marcia

Leon Jessel

# Parade of the Toy Soldiers

Primo

Leon Jessel

Tempo di Marcia

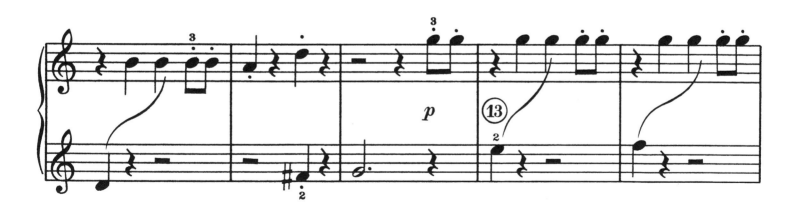

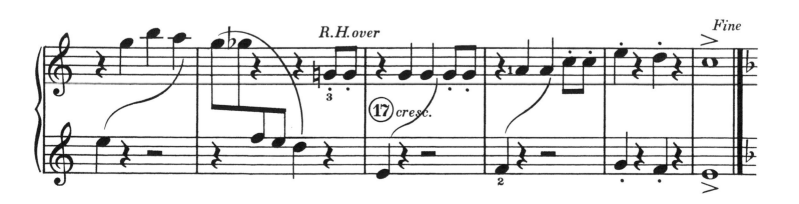

Parade of the Toy Soldiers - continued

SECONDO

D.C. al Fine

Parade of the Toy Soldiers – continued

*PRIMO*

# Successful Schaum Sheet Music
## This is a Partial List — Showing Level 1 through Level 2

✋= 5 Finger Position   * = Big Notes   • = Original Form   ✓ = Chord Symbols

### ACTION SOLOS
| | | | LEVEL |
|---|---|---|---|
| 55-10 *• | ABOMINABLE SNOWMAN (Left Hand Melody) | Durocher | 2 |
| 52-07 *• | ASTRONAUT ADVENTURE (Left Hand Melody) | Schaum | 1 |
| 52-25 *• | BUBBLE BLUES | Weston | 1 |
| 55-20 * | POGO STICK CHOP (Based on "Chop Sticks") | Schaum | 2 |
| 55-34 • | RIGHT ON (Staccato) | Miller | 2 |
| 55-26 • | WATER SLIDE (Staccato) | Payne | 2 |

### AMERICAN – PATRIOTIC SOLOS
| | | | |
|---|---|---|---|
| 55-14 | AMERICA THE BEAUTIFUL | Ward | 2 |
| 55-41 | MARINES' HYMN | Traditional | 2 |
| 55-08 | WABASH CANNON BALL | Railroad Song | 2 |

### ANIMALS and BIRDS
| | | | |
|---|---|---|---|
| 52-08 *• | BLUE GNU ✋ (Minor Key) | Danford | 1 |
| 55-36 *✓ | BUSHY-TAILED SQUIRREL | Jones | 2 |
| 52-16 *• | BUSY WOODPECKER ✋ (Staccato) | Cahn | 1 |
| 52-29 • | BUZZY AND WUZZY (Two Kittens) | Maier | 1 |
| 52-36 • | DINOSAUR LAND | Schaum | 1 |
| 52-38 • | KANGAROO HOP ✋ | Polk | 1 |
| 52-24 *• | PERKY TURKEY | Weston | 1 |
| 55-09 *• | POPPO the PORPOISE (Left Hand Melody) | Littlewood | 2 |
| 55-11 • | SEAGULL (Left Hand Melody) | Newman | 2 |
| 55-33 • | TOMMY CAT | Jones | 2 |

### BOOGIE
| | | | |
|---|---|---|---|
| 55-07 *• | COOL SCHOOL (Boogie Style) | Schaum | 2 |
| 55-02 • | LITTLE DOG BOOGIE | Schaum | 2 |

### BOTH HANDS in TREBLE CLEF
| | | | |
|---|---|---|---|
| 52-27 • | JOYOUS BELLS ✋ (with Duet Accompaniment) | Cahn | 1 |
| 55-44 • | MYSTICAL ETUDE (Staccato) | Cahn | 2 |

### CHRISTMAS
| | | | |
|---|---|---|---|
| 70-10 * | IT CAME UPON THE MIDNIGHT CLEAR | Traditional | 1 |
| 81-01 *✓ | IT'S BEGINNING TO LOOK LIKE CHRISTMAS | | 2 |
| 81-06 | LITTLE DRUMMER BOY, The | Arr. Schaum | 1 |
| 70-02 | TWELVE DAYS of CHRISTMAS | All 12 Verses | 1 |
| 70-01 * | WHAT CHILD IS THIS? ("Greensleeves") | Traditional | 1 |

### CIRCUS
| | | | |
|---|---|---|---|
| 55-39 • | CIRCUS PONIES | Leach | 2 |
| 55-19 *• | JOLLY CLOWN | Weston | 2 |

### CLASSICS
| | | | |
|---|---|---|---|
| 52-09 * | Beethoven | SONG of JOY ("Ode To Joy" from 9th Symph.) | 1 |
| 52-37 | Grieg | In the HALL of the MOUNTAIN KING | 1 |
| 52-12 ✓ | Handel | HALLELUJAH CHORUS (Easy Edition) | 1 |
| 55-30 | Mozart | MOZART'S ROMANCE (from "A Little Night Music") | 2 |
| 55-45 | Pachelbel | PACHELBEL'S CANON (Easy Edition) | 2 |
| 52-35 | Rossini | WILLIAM TELL MARCH | 1 |

### COUNTRY/WESTERN
| | | | |
|---|---|---|---|
| 55-35 | DAGGER DANCE ("Land of Sky Blue Waters") | Herbert | 2 |
| 52-06 *• | PONY RIDE ✋ | McCreary | 1 |
| 52-05 *• | TUMBLEWEED TRAIL | Frantz | 1 |

### DESCRIPTIVE MUSIC
| | | | |
|---|---|---|---|
| 52-39 • | ANCIENT PAGODA | Biel | 1 |
| 52-17 *• | CHARM BRACELET | Cahn | 1 |
| 55-46 • | COME BACK TO SORRENTO | deCurtis | 2 |
| 55-47 • | DOMINOES | Cahn | 2 |
| 52-32 *• | GLIDING ON THE WIND | Hampton | 1 |
| 55-49 • | IN A FAR OFF TIME & PLACE | Revezoulis | 2 |
| 52-40 • | JOLLY LEPRECHAUN | Revezoulis | 1 |
| 55-51 • | PEACEFUL INTERLUDE | Holmes | 2 |
| 55-37 • | PICTURE POSTCARD (w/Duet Accompaniment) | Cahn | 2 |
| 52-14 *• | SLUMBER PARTY | Stecker | 1 |
| 55-42 • | SUNSET SERENADE | Levin | 2 |

### DISSONANCE
| | | | LEVEL |
|---|---|---|---|
| 55-32 • | ROBOT TALK (Staccato) | Cray | 2 |
| 55-27 • | VIDEO GAME (Staccato) | Russell/Schaum | 2 |

### DUET (1 Piano, 4 Hands)
| | | | |
|---|---|---|---|
| 71-02 | PARADE of the TOY SOLDIERS | Jessel | 1 |
| 71-07 | HARK the HERALD ANGELS SING | Traditional | 2 |

### FOOD
| | | | |
|---|---|---|---|
| 55-38 • | HURRY, LITTLE PIZZA CAR | Holmes | 2 |

### HALLOWEEN
| | | | |
|---|---|---|---|
| 55-40 *• | GALLOPING GHOSTS (Minor Key) | Weston/Schaum | 2 |
| 52-15 *• | SPOOK HOUSE (Left Hand Melody) | Schaum | 1 |
| 52-20 *• | SPUNKY SPOOKS (Both Hands in Bass) | Weston | 1 |

### JAZZ STYLE
| | | | |
|---|---|---|---|
| 55-48 • | DUDE | Weston | 2 |

### LEFT HAND MELODY
| | | | |
|---|---|---|---|
| 52-22 • | KNOCKING AT MY DOOR ✋ | Schaum | 1 |
| 52-03 *• | LUMBERJACK SONG | Schaum | 1 |
| 55-50 • | SCOTTISH SKETCH | Holmes | 2 |

### MARCHES
| | | | |
|---|---|---|---|
| 52-34 • | FANFARE | King | 1 |
| 52-23 • | HAPPY FINGERS ✋ | Barrett | 1 |
| 55-06 | PARADE of the TOY SOLDIERS | Jessel | 2 |

### MINOR KEY
| | | | |
|---|---|---|---|
| 52-28 • | SECRET AGENT | Weston | 1 |

### MOVIE THEME
| | | | |
|---|---|---|---|
| 80-01 | STAR WARS (Main Title) | Williams | 2 |

### OLDIES but GOODIES
| | | | |
|---|---|---|---|
| 52-02 * | IN MY MERRY OLDSMOBILE | Edwards | 1 |
| 52-21 ✓ | SCHOOL DAYS | Edwards | 1 |

### RAGTIME
| | | | |
|---|---|---|---|
| 55-21 *✓ | ENTERTAINER (Easy Version) | Joplin | 2 |

### SACRED
| | | | |
|---|---|---|---|
| 55-25 *✓ | HOW GREAT THOU ART | Swedish Folk Melody | 2 |

### SPORTS
| | | | |
|---|---|---|---|
| 52-10 *• | CHEERLEADER | Plank | 1 |
| 52-18 *• | JOGGING TRAIL ✋ (Minor Key) | Payne | 1 |
| 52-19 *• | PEDAL BOAT | Schaum | 1 |
| 55-43 • | ROLLER BLADES | Schaum | 2 |
| 55-16 • | SKY DIVING (Broken Chords) | Newman | 2 |
| 55-28 ✓ | TAKE ME OUT TO THE BALL GAME | Von Tilzer | 2 |

### SPRINGTIME
| | | | |
|---|---|---|---|
| 55-18 *• | FAWN'S LULLABY | Masson | 2 |
| 55-03 • | JUMPING ROPE | Schaum | 2 |
| 52-04 * | SPRING, SWEET SPRING | Lincke | 1 |
| 52-31 *• | TREES IN THE BREEZE | Hampton | 1 |

### STACCATO
| | | | |
|---|---|---|---|
| 55-23 *• | FRISKY FROG (Both Hands in Treble) | Cahn | 2 |
| 52-33 • | HOPSCOTCH | Hampton | 1 |
| 52-11 *• | WINDSHIELD WIPER ROCK (Staccato) | Noblitt | 1 |

### THANKSGIVING
| | | | |
|---|---|---|---|
| 52-24 *• | PERKY TURKEY | Weston | 1 |
| 55-12 | THANKSGIVING SCENE | Medley of 4 Hymns | 2 |

### WALTZES
| | | | |
|---|---|---|---|
| 52-30 • | OPUS ONE | Cahn | 1 |